A Book of Signs

The Miraculous Signs in
The Gospel of John

By Brian Sherring

ISBN: 978-1-78364-564-0

www.obt.org.uk

****

The Open Bible Trust
Fordland Mount, Upper Basildon,
Reading, RG8 8LU, UK.

www.obt.org.uk

A Book of Signs

The Miraculous Signs in The Gospel of John

Contents

Page

The Structure of The Eight Signs in John's Gospel

A The Wedding at Cana—"they have no wine" (v.3) 2:1-11.

  B The Ruler's Son—he was "at the point of death" (v.47) 4:46-54.

    C The Invalid—he "had been an invalid for 38 years" (v.5) 5:1-18.

      Da The Feeding of 5000—"buy bread that these people may eat" (v.5) 6:1-15.

        E Walking on the water—"It is I, do not be afraid" (v.20) 6:16-21.

      Db The Feeding of the 5000—"I am the bread of life"(v.35) 6:22-59.

    C The Man born Blind—"blind from birth" (v.1) 9:1-41

  B The Raising of Lazarus—"Lazarus is dead" (v.14) 11:1-44.

A The Draught of fish—"they caught nothing" (v.3) 21:1-14.

1. Preliminary observations

For many, the Gospel of John is the best loved of the four Gospels. When I was a young Christian, it was recommended to me as a good starting point for the study of the New Testament. With hindsight, and with a bit more knowledge of the Scriptures than I had then, I think there is room for doubt about this view.

The Synoptic Gospels

The priority for anyone approaching the New Testament Scriptures for the first time, must be to get a good grasp of the narrative that is just as much part of the Synoptics accounts (Matthew Mark and Luke) concerning Jesus of Nazareth, as it is in John.

In fact, in Matthew and Luke, not only do we read additionally of His birth and early life, but we have His genealogy, and that is important in establishing His human origin and descent "according to the flesh" (Romans 9:5; cp. Philippians 2:6-8; Hebrews 2:14).

The Purpose for Writing

All the New Testament writings were written with some purpose in view. Whatever relevance they may have to us today, it is important to discover (if possible) first of all what that original purpose was.

With some books it is obvious; see Luke 1:1-4 for instance. He wrote so that Theophilus would know with 'certainty' events concerning Jesus of Nazareth.

And it is equally important to know to whom they were written: see James 1:1; 1 Peter 1;1 & 2 Peter 3:1. These all wrote to the Jews of the dispersion.

And, if possible, it is important to know the circumstances under which they were 'penned'. For example, Paul's Corinthian letters seem to have been 'sparked off' by a report sent to him from "the house of Chloe", concerning the divisions and behaviour of some within the Corinthian church (1 Corinthians 1:10-13).

The Reason John Wrote

In the case of the Gospel of John, he states that he has recorded a selected number of "signs" from "the innumerable signs" that Jesus did "in the presence of His disciples," to convince his readers that:

> Jesus is the Christ (Messiah), the Son of God, and that by believing you may have life in his name. (John 20:31)

This was why he wrote his Gospel; this was the goal he hoped to achieve. Before we ask the question, "Why these particular *signs*?" let us look at these two verses in detail.

Jesus is the Christ

I have noticed that some Christians reading these verses, place more emphasis on the second of these two clauses —"by believing you may have life in his name". However, this is to gloss over the claim made in the first clause—namely that "Jesus is the Christ".

John is not urging his readers to believe **in** Jesus Christ, but primarily to believe, based upon the "signs" he has recorded, that "Jesus **is** the Christ (Messiah)".

And he draws attention to the fact (again not always noted as of too much importance) that these "signs" were done "*in the presence of*" Jesus' disciples.

This could suggest that many of these disciples were still alive when John wrote this Gospel, who could substantiate John's "signs".

Compare this with the way the Apostle Paul wrote his first letter to the Corinthians. He was able to refer to "five hundred brethren ... *most of whom are still alive*", who could witness to the fact that Jesus had risen from the dead (1 Corinthians 15:6)).

If Jesus' disciples were still living, and so were supportive witnesses, then it suggests an early date for the Gospel. John was writing to his own generation living during the Acts period, urging his brethren to accept Jesus as the Messiah. And that may have determined which "signs" John chose to include in his Gospel.

Dating John's Gospel

The suggestion that John wrote his Gospel whilst an old man during the reign of Domitian (A.D. 81-96), and over fifty years after the events that he records in his Gospel, is quite popular amongst some commentators, but there is no compelling reason why it should be so. It is based upon tradition, and as John A.T. Robinson noted:

> That John wrote as a very old man is an inference which

only appears late and accompanied by statements which show that it is clearly secondary and unreliable. (*Redating the New Testament*)

That John lived to a great age is a strong tradition, but that he waited some fifty odd years after the events he records in his Gospel, before he put them in writing, is, as Robinson notes, "unreliable". And when we come to look at the reason he wrote it, and its original destination, a very late date makes no sense at all.

The Destruction of the Temple

An observation that is rarely commented upon, is that not one of the New Testament writings, including John's Gospel, shows any sign that the destruction of Jerusalem and the Temple (A.D.70) had already taken place. They prophesy of it (e.g. Matthew 24:1,2) but give no hint that it had happened when they wrote.

Both James Moffatt (translator of the Bible version that bears his name) and John A.T. Robinson (author of *Redating the New Testament* and *The Priority of John*) made this observation many years ago.

Also, nearer to home, for a detailed look at the early dating of the Gospel, readers might like to refer to the appendix in Michael Penny's *Approaching the Bible* and the present author's *The Gospel of John and the Samaritans*, both obtainable from The Open Bible Trust.

John's Gospel is Jewish

The dating of John's Gospel and its subject matter is important to these studies. That the Gospel is essentially Jewish in nature was noted in the 19th Century by J.B. Lightfoot who wrote:

> It is the most Hebraic book in the New Testament, except perhaps the Apocalypse. (*Biblical Essays*).

Lightfoot's overall analysis of the Gospel is well worth repeating here, setting the Gospel within the background against which it was first written, and John's purpose in writing it in the first place. Following his observation quoted above, he wrote:

> The Messianic idea is turned about on all sides, and presented in every aspect. On this point we learn more of contemporary Jewish opinion from the Fourth Gospel than from the other three. At the commencement and at the close of the narrative—in the preaching of the Baptist and in the incidents of the Passion—it is equally prominent. In Galilee in Samaria, in Judea, it is the one standard theme of conversation. Among friends, among foes, among neutrals alike it is mooted and discussed. The person and character of Jesus are tried by this standard. He is accepted or He is rejected, as He fulfils or contradicts the received ideal of the Messiah. (*Biblical Essays*)

Another much respected 19th century scholar, B.F. Westcott wrote,

> Without the basis of the Old Testament, without the acceptance of the unchanging divinity of the Old Testament, the Gospel of St. John is an insoluble riddle. (*Gospel according to St. John*).

The belief, therefore, that the Gospel of John is a suitable starting point for the young Christian to study the New Testament, is thrown into doubt when we realise, as Wescott noted (above), that "Without the basis of the Old Testament ... the Gospel of St. John is an insoluble riddle."

The primary aim of the Fourth Gospel, as John claims, is to prove that "Jesus is the Messiah, the Son of God", and it was addressed to those for whom that was a vital question to be answered. And it is against that background that John presents his "signs".

2. Signs and Miracles

In the first chapter I noted that John's primary reason for 'penning' his Gospel was summed up in the words of 20:31, "That you may believe that Jesus is the Messiah, the Son of God." And he promised his readers on that basis, "life in his name".

The promise of "life in his name" is, of course, relevant for all who believe in Jesus Christ, Jew and Gentile, but the difference in John's Gospel is that he is urging his readers to believe that Jesus **is** the Messiah. He is asking them to accept that Jesus of Nazareth is the one promised to the people of Israel in Old Testament times.

To a Jew, Jesus was, and still is, a name and Messiah is a title; to a Gentile, especially today, "Jesus Christ" has become a name.

To those first disciples who heard John the Baptist's testimony to Jesus as "The Lamb of God who takes away the sin of the world", Jesus was recognised:

- By Andrew as "the Messiah".
- By Philip as "him of whom Moses in the Law and also the prophets wrote, Jesus of Nazareth, the son of Joseph".
- By Nathanael as "the Son of God... the King of Israel" (John 1:29, 40, 41, 45, 49).

The Messiah and The Prophet

Messiah was a character who existed in Jewish prophecy long before He came in Person to the earth. Following John the

Baptist's declaration that he came baptising—"that he (Jesus, the Son of God) might be revealed to Israel" (1:31,34)—these three disciples gave their own testimony to Him as the long awaited Messiah, King of Israel and The Prophet of whom Moses spoke (Deuteronomy 18:15,18,19).

In Jewish thinking at the time, "the Prophet" seems to have been distinguished from the Messiah, but Peter identified Him as one and the same as Jesus of Nazareth (Acts 3:19-22. cp. 7:37; John 1:21,25; 6:14; 7:40).

And as Lightfoot observed in his analysis of John's Gospel, the whole of the narrative revolves round the Old Testament standard of whether "Jesus of Nazareth is accepted or He is rejected, as He fulfils or contradicts the received ideal of the Messiah" (*Biblical Essays*).

Signs and miracles

John does not describe the wonders of Jesus the Messiah as "miracles" (*dunamis*) as such. In his Gospel, to him they are "signs"; Greek *semeion*. It is not that the other Evangelists do not use the word, in fact, chronologically, the first use of it is in Luke 2:12, where the shepherds were told by the angel of the Lord of the birth of the Messiah, and the "sign" (*semeion)* given them was, "you will find a baby wrapped in swaddling clothes and lying in a manger."

But its usage in John is significant, in that his Gospel was written around specific "signs" to demonstrate "that you may believe that Jesus is the Messiah" (John 20:31). Who the "you" were, we will have to explore more fully.

Miraculous Signs

The word *semeion* is used 17 times in John's Gospel (13 in Matthew; 7 in Mark and 10 in Luke). It is used in ten of the twenty-one chapters of John, firstly of the changing of water into wine (2:1-11).

Then, in Jerusalem, following His 'driving out' of the money changers in the temple, Jesus was asked by the Jews, "What *sign* do you show us for doing these things?", (John 2:18). To this he replied: "Destroy this temple, and in three days I will raise it up".

These words, taken literally by the Jews, and not understood by the disciples at the time, only became clear to them when they were fulfilled by the Messiah's resurrection (John 2:18-22; cp. 20:9).

The Greatest Sign

The Lord's rising from the dead is in fact the greatest "sign" of all. He called it, "the sign of Jonah", who was symbolically raised from the dead when delivered from the belly of the great fish.

It was the only "sign" He offered to "an evil and adulterous generation", largely represented by the scribes, Pharisees and Sadducees (Matthew 16:1,4). They stood condemned by the men of Nineveh who "repented at the preaching of Jonah" unlike the current generation's reaction to the teaching of their Messiah, one far greater than Jonah (Matthew 12:38-42).

Later, in contrast, whilst Jesus was in Jerusalem during the Passover feast, it is used of the "signs" He did there, with the result that "many believed in his name"; (John 2:23).

Healings

Nicodemus acknowledges Jesus as a Rabbi (teacher) because, "no one can do these *signs* unless God is with him" (John 3:1,2), and when called upon to heal the ruler's son—who was "at the point of death"—Jesus bemoans the fact that "Unless you (people) see *signs* and wonders you will not believe". This was "the second *sign* that Jesus did when he had come from Judea to Galilee" (John 4:46-54).

In 5:1-18 John records the healing of a man who "had been an invalid for 38 years" (v.5), and although the word "sign" is not mentioned here, this is clearly the third sign that John is referring to.

By the Sea of Tiberias, Jesus was followed by a large crowd, "because they saw the *signs* he was doing on the sick"; (John 6:2). This led to the fourth "sign"—the Feeding of the Five Thousand (6:1-14).

Feeding 5,000 and Walking on Water

This 'miracle' of producing enough bread and fish from "five barley loaves and two fish" to feed such a large company, was seen by the people as a "sign" that Jesus was "*the* Prophet who is to come into the world" (John 6:14). But Jesus, perceiving that the crowd were about to take him by force to make him king, "withdrew again to the mountain by himself" (v.15). Here John records the fifth sign— the 'miracle' of Jesus walking on water— meeting up with His disciples on the lake (6:16-21), again not referred to as a "sign" but it evidently was.

Jesus then encounters the crowd who follow Him to Capernaum.

He said to them, "Truly, truly, I say to you, you are seeking me, not because you saw "signs", but because you had your fill of the loaves."

And when asked by them, "What must we do, to be doing the works of God?" He answered, "This is the work of God, that you believe in him whom he has sent" (John 6:25-29). It beggars belief that, after all they had seen and heard over the last few days they said to Him, "What *sign* do you do, that we may see and believe you?" (John 6:30).

The Messiah and Signs

In chapter 7, Jesus is back in Jerusalem where the "authorities" sought to arrest Him, "but no one laid a hand on him, because his hour had not yet come", and "many of the people believed in him". And they pondered, "When the Messiah appears, will he do more *signs* than this man has done?" (John 7:25-31).

In Jerusalem again, we have the sixth "sign"—the healing of the man born blind (John 9:1-41)—which, because it was on the Sabbath, led to some of the Pharisees condemning Jesus and saying, "This man is not from God, for he does not keep the Sabbath". This caused a "division" amongst them, for other Pharisees noted, "How can a man who is a sinner do such *signs*?" (John 9:13-16).

The Testimony of John

The next reference to "signs" follows the Lord's fleeing from an attempt on His life when He claimed, "I and the Father are one". The Jews interpreted this as "making himself God," and set about to stone Him.

Escaping from their hands, He went to "the place where John had been baptising at first, and there he remained." Many came to him, and said, "John did no *sign*, but everything that John said about this man was true. And many believed in him there"; John 10:22-42.

This is the one place where *semeion* is used, where I feel that the *KJV* makes the point more effectively by translating, "John did no miracle" (v.41).

Lazarus

The Raising of Lazarus (John 11:1-44), was an event that was to have reverberations. He was a living testimony to the power and authority of Jesus, and many "who had been present when (Jesus) called Lazarus out of the tomb and raised him from the dead *continued to bear witness*".

But, the chief priests had already made plans to put Lazarus to death, "on account that many of the Jews were going away and believing in Jesus" (John 12:9-11).

Nevertheless, on Christ's triumphal entry into Jerusalem (itself a "sign"; John 12:14; Zechariah 9:9), a crowd had gone out to meet the Lord, "because they had heard that He had done *this sign*" (John 12:12-18). The raising of Lazarus was the apostle John's seventh "sign."

Jews Demand a Sign

The above references to "signs" in John's Gospel show clearly what Paul was later to observe in his first letter to the Corinthians—"*Jews demand signs* and Greeks seek wisdom" (1

Corinthians 1:22)—and John in his efforts to convince his brethren that Jesus of Nazareth was their Messiah, has given them a sample of the many signs that Jesus did in the presence of His disciples (John 20:30,31) .

3. The last chapter and the eighth sign

John has recorded *seven* specific signs in the first twenty chapters of his Gospel. This does not include the Lord's resurrection, which is the greatest "sign" of all (Matthew 12:38-40). John chapter 21 ends with John's reason for writing his Gospel:

> Now Jesus did many other *signs* in the presence of his disciples, which are not written in this book; but these are written so that you may believe that Jesus is the Messiah, the Son of God, and that by believing you may have life in his name. (John 20:30-31).

An afterthought?

At this point, many commentators believe the Gospel of John originally ended, and that chapter 21 was 'an afterthought'. And "this distinction is no refinement of modern theorists; it is as old as the time of Tertullian" (A.D. 160?—230?). And that this 'afterthought' was written by the apostle John is well authenticated, by tradition and by the observation that "the style is essentially Johannine" (J.B. Lightfoot *Biblical Essays*).

When it was added is impossible to say, but as Lightfoot further noted, "there is nothing in the style which requires us to postulate more than a few weeks or a few days. All the manuscripts without exception contain the chapter, and there is no trace of its ever having been wanting from any copies".

The reason

Why it was added can be gleaned from its content, which is largely about Peter and John ("the disciple whom Jesus loved" (13:23; 21:7,20). John had recorded Peter as having denied his Lord three times (18:17,25,27); now he records that the Lord gave him three opportunities to exonerate himself— "Simon ... do you love me ... love me ... love me" (vs.15-19)

And, in response to Peter's question regarding John's 'fate', John wants to 'clear up' a misunderstanding concerning a belief that had arisen about the Lord's answer to that question, that he, John, would not die but remain until the return of the Lord. John says he was not given such a guarantee: the Lord had said, "**If** it is my will that he remain ... what is that to you Peter?" (vs.20-23).

An eighth sign

But also recorded in chapter 21, is what is sometimes taken as an *eighth sign*, even though the apostle does not refer to it as such— The Draught of Fish—an event that John sums up as, "This was now the third time that Jesus was revealed to the disciples after he was raised from the dead" (21:1-14). And he closes this 'second end' of his Gospel with the words:

> Now there are many other *things* that Jesus did. Were every one of them to be written, I suppose that the world itself could not contain the books that would be written. (John 21:25)

So, was the large quantity of fish (153, v.11) caught by the disciples under the Lord's instruction, who up until then had "caught nothing" (v.3), an eighth "sign"? Was it a 'miracle?' Let us examine the detail of the event.

Was it a miracle?

The disciples were in their boat on the Sea of Tiberius and had fished all night and caught nothing. At daybreak they came near to the shore where Jesus was standing, although they did not at this point recognise Him.

He asked them, "Do you have any fish"? Their answer was "No". He instructed them to cast their net "on the right side of the boat", and then they were not able to haul in the net because of the quantity of fish in it" (v.6). Wherein lies the miracle'?

Did the Lord create these fish, or were they already there, and hence the 'miracle' simply involved 'knowing where they were?'

It is well known, especially to fishermen, that fish gather in shoals, and often swim together in the same direction in a coordinated manner. Some 'shoal' or 'school' all their lives, and they do so for various reasons; enhanced foraging success, better predator detection and finding a mate. Hence one can fish in one place and get little or nothing, but just a very short distance away fish are to be had in quantity.

Is it a 'miracle' to know where a shoal of fish is? An experienced fisherman could probably find them without recourse to a 'miracle', and the disciples here were fishermen. But was it a "sign" in the sense that the other seven were?

Was it a sign?

It is evident that a "sign" does not have to be a "miracle", although there are places where they evidently were, especially in John's Gospel. All the seven "signs" John records in the first twenty chapters of his Gospel are evidently 'miracles', but would we consider speaking in tongues a 'miracle?' Paul calls it a "sign" (1 Corinthians 14:22). And a distinction is made in Acts 8:13 where we read that Simon the magician was amazed, "seeing signs (*semeia*) and great miracles (*dunameis*) performed".

So, is the Draught of Fishes in chapter 21 an eighth "sign", even though it is not described as such by John, and is recorded in a context where John refers to "many other *things* (not 'signs') that Jesus did"?

I will come back to this event in a later chapter, including why John records that the fish numbered 153 (v.11), but for now I take it to be a "sign", and just as much 'written' for the same reason as the other seven—"that you may believe that Jesus is the Messiah, the Son of God"—if only on the basis of its place in the overall structure of the other "signs".

The Structure of
The Eight Signs in John's Gospel

A The Wedding at Cana—"they have no wine" (v.3) 2:1-11.

B The Ruler's Son—he was "at the point of death" (v.47) 4:46-54.

C The Invalid—he "had been an invalid for 38 years" (v.5) 5:1-18.

   Da The Feeding of 5000—"buy bread that these people may eat" (v.5) 6:1-15.

     E Walking on the water—"It is I, do not be afraid" (v.20) 6:16-21.

   Db The Feeding of the 5000—"I am the bread of life" (v.35) 6:22-59.

C The Man born Blind—"blind from birth" (v.1) 9:1-41

B The Raising of Lazarus—"Lazarus is dead" (v.14) 11:1-44.

A The Draught of fish—"they caught nothing" (v.3) 21:1-14.

The structure above is an abbreviated copy of the very detailed form in which it occurs in *The Companion Bible* Appendix 176. In that publication, where the "signs" are set out in parallel form, the case for there being eight and not seven "signs", is even more compelling than I am able to present it in this short book. To leave the Draught of fish out of the that structure, would upset the balance of John's "signs", as presented to us by him.

In the next chapters I take an overview of these signs as set out in the above structure, and try to answer the question why John picked these particular "signs" in writing his Gospel.

One thing is certain, that what John recorded of the first sign, is true of all: "The first of his signs—turning water into wine—Jesus did at Cana in Galilee, and *manifested his glory*. And his disciples believed in him.".

4. Eight Signs: An Overview

The *prime* object stated by John as to why he recorded the "signs" that he did, must always be kept before our minds.

> Now Jesus did many other *signs* in the presence of his disciples, which are not written in this book; but these are written *so that you may believe that Jesus is the Messiah, the Son of God.* (John 20:30,31)

This statement is often passed over by Gentiles, who hurry on to the second clause, "and that by believing you may have life in his name."

A Jew would be challenged by associating Jesus, a name, with Messiah, a title, but generally, not a Gentile. Even unbelieving Gentiles accept Jesus Christ as a name, without ever considering the implications of joining the two together, which would trouble a Jew.

Whatever we make of the "signs" John relates in his Gospel, they must be seen against the background of his statement at the end of chapter 20. And so, in this overview of the eight signs, I will keep that always in mind.

B.F. Westcott in his *Gospel According to John*, wrote:

> Without the basis of the Old Testament, without the acceptance of the unchanging divinity of the Old Testament, the Gospel of St. John is an insoluble riddle.

That may seem rather a strong statement, but when we consider how often the New Testament writers refer to the Old Testament—"It is written", "It stands in Scripture", "As Isaiah predicted" etc.—it is quite evident that, to some of the Jews at least, the things that were happening during the Gospel and Acts periods were related to prophecies in the Hebrew Scriptures.

Peter, as well as John

And John in his Gospel, was particularly concerned with showing that the "signs", (miracles) that were done by Jesus, were the 'signs of the Messiah'. And he was not the only apostle who appealed to such signs. Peter, speaking to "Men of Israel", referred his hearers to:

> "Jesus of Nazareth, a man *attested to you by God* with mighty works and wonders and *signs* that God did through him in your midst, as you yourselves know." (Acts 2:22)

The expectations of the Jews concerning the Messiah at this time, were met in Jesus insofar that He was a descendant of David and born in Bethlehem (Micah 5:2; John 7:42). And it was expected that the Messiah would be a 'greater Moses'; the Jews said to Jesus,

> "What sign do you do, that we may see and believe you? What work do you perform? Our fathers ate the manna in the wilderness; as it is written, 'He (Moses) gave them bread from heaven to eat.'" (John 6:30,31)

So, we can imagine the ferment occasioned by the feeding of the five thousand, when the people saw that "sign" and said, "This is indeed the Prophet who is to come into the world!" and which led them to try and "take him by force to make him king", (John

6:14,15). But Jesus withdrew to a mountain by himself.

This "sign", based upon Jewish expectations, convinced some, but when in the Lord's subsequent discourse, He claimed to be "the bread of life" with all its implications, "many of his disciples turned back and no longer walked with him" (6:35-66). As with all the "signs", I will look again at this "sign" later: my point here is that the signs that John chose to convince his readers that Jesus of Nazareth was indeed the promised Messiah, had their root in the Hebrew Scriptures, and Jewish expectation.

Water to Wine and The Draft of Fish

These two "signs" appear in parallel in the above structure; both speaking of something lacking—'they have no wine', 'they caught no fish', but in what way do they testify to Jesus as the Messiah? What is the common factor?

It is easy to come up with a number of answers. I suggest that the overriding factor is to present the reader with the very first statement concerning the Word who was made flesh—He is the Creator—"All things were made through him, and without him was not anything made that was made", (John 1:3).

Both "signs" demonstrate that Jesus, as the Word, was the Creator and Provider, and "the Word became flesh and dwelt among us", in local terms … amongst the Jews, but in the wider picture ... in the world.

The Ruler's Son and The Raising of Lazarus

The common factor here is death and resurrection, the Ruler's son was "at the point of death", seemingly beyond human help, but was delivered from it at the last moment by the word of Jesus alone; no need to visit his bedside. And the Official believed the promise of Jesus—"Go, your son will live" and went on his way (John 4:46-54).

We could compare this event with the deliverance of Isaac from the knife that Abraham wielded as he prepared to sacrifice Isaac, who was at that moment, 'at the point of death' (Genesis 22:1-14).

And compare the Hebrew writer's interpretation of this story where he saw Isaac as "figuratively ... *raised from the dead*", (Hebrews 11:17-19).

In the case of Lazarus, he had actually died—"Lazarus is dead" (John 11:14). This is emphasised in verse 17 where we are told that when Jesus came to him, "he had been four days in the tomb." Martha was confident that "he will rise again in the resurrection on the last day", but Jesus said to her, "I am the resurrection and the life. Whoever believes in me, though he die, yet shall he live" (John 11:24,25), and hence when He stood by the tomb Jesus cried out, "Lazarus, come out", and "the man who had died came out"; not a ghost, but flesh and blood.

It is no wonder that "the chief priests made plans to put Lazarus to death"; he was a living example to the Lord's power over death, and many came to Bethany (near Jerusalem) at the time of the Passover, not just to see Jesus, but "also to see Lazarus",

(12:1,9-11).

The Invalid and The Man born Blind

With the possible exception of The Feeding of the 5000 and its connection with Moses, the most obvious and predicted "signs" of the Messiah involved healing.

When Jesus stood up in the synagogue in Nazareth to read from Isaiah 61:1,2, He read of, "the year of the Lord's favour" and said of it, "Today, this Scripture has been fulfilled in your hearing".

And one of the "signs" associated with this time was, "*the recovering of sight to the blind*" (Luke 4:16-21). In another place, Isaiah had prophesied of the coming of God to recompense and save His people and said, "Then the eyes of *the blind* shall be opened ... *the lame* man shall leap like a deer" (Isaiah 35:4-6).

Of John the Baptist, it was prophesied, "He shall be filled with the Holy Spirit, even from his mother's womb" (Luke 1:15) and the Lord testified of him, "Among those born of women none is greater than John" (Luke 7:28), and yet he seems, at one point in his witness, to have had some doubts about who Jesus was. Did he experience a 'blip' in his faith?

Had he not testified to the early disciples that Jesus was "the Lamb of God", "the Son of God"? Now he sends two of his disciples to ask Him, "Are you the one who is to come, or shall we look for another? Whilst those disciples were with Jesus, He healed many people in their presence, and He sent them back to John with this message:

"Go and tell John what you have seen and heard: t*he blind*

receive their sight, the lame walk, lepers are cleansed, and the deaf hear, the dead are raised up..." (Luke 7:18-23)

These were the credentials of the Messiah and they are two of the Apostle John's "signs" to 'prove' that "Jesus is the Messiah, the Son of God"—The Invalid that was able to walk and The Blind Man that was able to see.

Feeding of the 5000 and Walking on Water

These are the only two 'miracles' which John records in common with the other three Gospels, where they occur in Matthew 14:13-33; Mark 6:32-44 and Luke 9:10-17. The Feeding of the 5000 is described in John 6:1-14 and the Lord's teaching based on the event continues at 6:22-59. Between these Jesus retires to a mountain for some respite, and returns to meet up with the disciples again on the lake. But he meets them in a miraculous way, Walking on the Water. We can set it out within the structure of all John's "signs" like this:

> **Da** The Feeding of 5000—"buy bread that these people
> may eat" (v.5) 6:1-15.
> **E** Walking on the water "It is I, do not be afraid"
> (v.20) 6:16-21.
> **Db** The Feeding of the 5000 "I am the bread of life"
> (v.35) 6:22-59.

Feeding of the 5000

The Feeding of the 5000 is at the very centre of John's Gospel, and draws a comparison between Moses the Lawgiver and the 'greater than Moses', the Messiah. We have already been introduced by John at the very beginning of his Gospel to this comparison: "the law was given through *Moses*; grace and truth came through *Jesus the Messiah*" (1:17).

After the 'miracle' where Jesus turned five barley loaves and two fish into enough food to feed a crowd of 5000, a comparison was made between that and Moses feeding the people of Israel in the wilderness with manna.

It seems almost unbelievable that those who saw the miracle and "ate their fill of the loaves", should then ask Jesus, "What *sign* do you do, that we may see and believe you? What work do you perform?", (6:26,30).

And they went on to say, citing Nehemiah 9:15: "Our fathers ate the manna in the wilderness as it is written, 'He gave them bread from heaven to eat.'" Jesus reminds them that it was not Moses who gave them "bread from heaven, but my Father gives you the true bread from heaven", which He defines as:

> The bread of God is he who comes down from heaven and gives life to the world ... I am the bread of life, whoever comes to me shall not hunger, and whoever believes in me shall never thirst. (6:32-35)

But the teaching of Jesus following The Feeding of the 5000, proved to be the catalyst that led to many who had followed Jesus after this event and to say, "This is a hard saying; who can listen to it?" and to "turn back and no longer walk with Jesus", (6:60,66). But there were those who said to the Lord, "To whom shall we go? You have the words of eternal life" (6:68,69).

Later, during the Acts period, many of the Jews, even amongst those who accepted Jesus as Messiah, struggled with the place of the Law in relation to the way of salvation. In Acts 15 this came to a head when a council was called to try and resolve the matter, especially in respect of those who were saying, "Unless you are circumcised according to the custom of Moses, you cannot be saved" (v.1). Circumcision was a commitment to keep the whole law, as Paul reminded the Galatians (Galatians 5:3).

Walking on Water

Between the actual event of The Feeding of the 5000 and the teaching of Jesus based upon it, which we might sum up in His claim, "I am the bread of life", we have the 'miracle' of His Walking on the Water during a strong wind and on a rough sea.

In Matthew's account of this 'miracle' (14:22-33) there are the added details of impetuous Peter, who, with the Lord's permission, attempted to 'walk on water' himself, but his faith was not sufficient, and Jesus had to rescue him. And, after Jesus had calmed the storm, those in the boat "worshipped him, saying, 'Truly you are the Son of God'" (v.33).

Mark has recorded what may be another occasion, how Jesus calmed a storm by rebuking the sea and saying to the wind, "Peace! Be still", which led to the disciples saying, "Who then is this, that even the wind and the sea obey him?", (Mark 4:39-41). All this demonstrates the Lord's command over the creation, and is one of the "signs" that show that Jesus is the Messiah, the Son of God (John 20:30,31).

*****

So ends a brief overview of the "signs" John presented to his readers, with the object that they, "may believe that Jesus is the Messiah, the Son of God", the first step to having, "life in his name".

In subsequent chapters I will go through these "signs" in more detail, and try to see why John picked these particular 'miracles' to convince his brethren to accept his testimony concerning Jesus.

5. The Wedding at Cana: Water into Wine

We might wonder why John did not pick a more spectacular "sign" as the first of his 'signs of the Messiah'. Compared to The Raising of Lazarus, for instance, it might seem a bit tame. But John obviously had his reasons.

We can, as many have done, speculate on the symbolic meaning of the "sign". Clement of Alexandria (150? — 220?) wrote of the Fourth Gospel, "John, perceiving that the external facts had been made plain in the (Synoptic) Gospels ... composed a *spiritual* Gospel".

Should we then try to find a 'spiritual' meaning behind every detail recorded in this "sign"? For example, it took place, "On the third day"; does that reflect in any way the resurrection of Jesus on the third day? I do not dismiss this as a possibility, but think a simpler explanation is better.

Jesus the Creator

Having revealed Jesus as the Word, maker of all things, made flesh, coming to His own people; and their reaction to Him, receiving Him or not (1:1-14), John sets out his early record of events in seven consecutive days.

Beginning with John the Baptist, whose activities had become significant enough for the authorities in Jerusalem to send a deputation to enquire of John, "Who are you?" (1:19), the record runs like this:

First Day:

Questioning of John by those sent from Jerusalem by the Pharisees—are you the Messiah ... Elijah ... the Prophet? The Baptist says "I am not" (1:19-28).

Second Day:

As Jesus comes towards him, John testifies to Him, "Behold, the Lamb of God who takes away the sin of the world" ... and having seen the Spirit descend upon Jesus, declares Him to be "the Son of God" (1:29-34).

Third Day:

The Baptist with two of his disciples, Andrew and (almost certainly) the apostle John, repeats his testimony to Jesus as "the Lamb of God." The two disciples follow Jesus and He asks them, "What are you seeking?" They say, "Rabbi, where are you staying", and He replies, "Come and you will see". They go with Him and stay with Jesus for that day (1:35-39).

Fourth Day:

As soon as the new day dawns, the first thing Andrew does is to find his brother, Simon, and he tells him, "We have found the Messiah". He brought him to Jesus who looks at this "Simon the son of John" and names him, Cephas (which means Peter) (1:40-42).

Fifth Day:

Jesus decides to go to Galilee. He finds Philip, who in turn finds Nathanael and says to him, "We have found him of whom Moses ... wrote, Jesus of Nazareth, the son of Joseph". Nathanael replies, "Can anything good come out of Nazareth?". Philip said to him, "Come and see".

Jesus seeing Nathanael, describes him as "An Israelite indeed", and when He further tells Nathanael of something in his past, this leads to him declaring Jesus as, "Rabbi, you are the Son of God! You are the king of Israel!"

Jesus, then promises this "Israelite indeed", a vision such as the first Israelite (Jacob) received, of "the angels of God ascending and descending on the Son of Man" (1:43-51; see Genesis 28:12).

Sixth Day:

Passed over in silence.

Seventh Day:

("The third day", i.e., two days after the promise to Nathanael), The Wedding at Cana (2:1-11).

Water into wine: The first Sign (2:1-11)

John does not record any discourse following this "sign" that might help us in determining the reason why he selected it.

It occurs in the normal course of events in the life of Jesus – He is invited to a wedding during which they ran out of wine. An embarrassment and serious matter for "the steward of the feast" – "without wine there is no joy" (old Jewish saying), but not 'life threatening'. The 'miracle' was that water was turned into a wine that was better than that which had been served up previously.

Analysing this in today's terms, many an amateur wine maker, with the help of some 'ingredients', can do the same. Apart from water, all that is required is a flavouring agent (fruit, berries, even grapes!), a fermenting substance, yeast, and a lot of time and patience.

The 'miracle' that Jesus did was to change water into wine, *instantaneously*. It demonstrated that He was the Creator, as John had already stated – "All things were made through him, and without him was not anything made that was made" (1:3).

John's account of this wedding, seen against the background of Jewish thinking and practices at the time, may reflect on them, without condemning them.

Six Water Jars

There were six water jars set there, "for the Jewish rites of purification, each holding twenty or thirty gallons."

If we take John's explanation of their purpose as *a reminder* to his Jewish readers, rather than as *an explanation* for non-Jewish readers, then John may be hinting here of "the nature and the weakness of Pharisaism" (*Tyndale N.T. Commentaaries,* R.V.G. Tasker).

The *six* jars of water, used for the ceremonial washing of hands and utensils (cp. Mark 7:3,4), may then represent the "law given by Moses" (1:17) or perhaps for John, more specifically, *the interpretation* of that law by the Pharisees. David H. Stern, in his *Jewish New Testament Commentary*, wrote,

> "'Cleansings' (Hebrew *Taharot*) is the title and subject of one of the **six** sections of the Talmud; *this is a measure of their importance in traditional Judaism.*"

And, as John himself records, even then, there were differences of interpretation about those 'cleansings'—"There arose a question between some of John's disciples and the Jews *about purifying*" (3:25).

In a Bad Sense

'Wine', in the Scriptures, has both bad and good connotations. In a bad sense wine can lead to drunkenness; wine brought evil in the drunkenness of Noah and the curse of Canaan (Genesis 9:20-25); drunkenness is one of "the works of the flesh" (Galatians 5:21) and is contrasted with being filled by the Holy Spirit in Ephesians 5:18.

In a Good Sense

In a good sense, wine gladdens the heart of man, and it was recommended to Timothy – "Drink no longer water, but use a little wine for your stomach's sake and often infirmities".

It even represents symbolically, the Messiah's "blood of the New Covenant" although John does not refer to it (Psalm 104:15; 1 Timothy 5:23; Luke 22;20).

But above all, for Israel, the building of vineyards and the drinking of wine is a feature of their future age of blessing (Jeremiah 31:4,5; Amos 9:13-15). Later in John's record, Jesus uses the allegory of the vine to declare, "I am the true vine" (15:1-5).

Why this Miracle?

So why did John select this 'miracle' as one of his signs to convince his brethren that "Jesus is the Christ, the Son of God"?

I said I looked for a simple answer, and so, instead of trying to 'spiritualise' every detail, and in view of there being no following discourse that bears upon it, I believe that John's purpose was simply to relate the first seven days of the Lord's ministry chronologically and, as he observes himself, "This, the first of his signs, Jesus did at Cana in Galilee, and *manifested his glory*. And his disciples believed in him (2:11).

6. The Ruler's Son: At the Point of Death

The background to the 'second sign' is the contrast between Jesus' reception in Nazareth, when He observed that "a prophet has no honour in his own home town", (Matthew 13:53-58) and when He came to Galilee where, "the Galileans welcomed him, having seen all that he had done in Jerusalem at the feast" (John 4:43-45).

This "second" of John's "signs" recorded in 4:46-54, took place when Jesus, "came again to Cana in Galilee, where he had made the water wine". Jesus had passed through Sychar and Samaria where he had met the Samaritan woman, and "*the* two days" (lit.) that He had spent with the Samaritans at their request, had passed (4:39-42). Now he encountered a man whose son was "at the point of death".

The Ruler's Son

The healing of The Ruler's Son has sometimes been seen as a variant of the account recorded in Luke 7:2-10 and Matthew 8:5-13, since in both cases the Lord healed 'at a distance', but this is improbable; there are too many differences between the accounts.

In John it is an Official's son who was healed; in Matthew and Luke, a Centurion's servant. Although the "faith" of those who called upon Jesus is uttermost in these 'miracles'.

The 'miracle' at Cana, when Jesus made water into wine, was

undoubtedly witnessed by many, and the story spread abroad. The Official in this second "sign" was prepared to make the twenty five mile journey from Capernaum as a last chance to save his son's life—"he was at the point of death"—on the basis that the 'miracle' was true.

He asked Jesus to return with him to cure his son, but when Jesus said to him, "Go, your son will live, he believed the word Jesus spoke to him and *went on his way*". It was subsequently established, that the fever left the Official's son at the very "hour" that the Lord had given the man His promise, and the man's faith, which had been strong enough to believe it, was further established, and "he himself believed, and all his household".

Signs and Wonders

When the Official first approached Jesus to heal his son, He said to the man, presumably in the presence of (many?) others, "Unless you see signs and wonders you will not believe" (4:48). John recalls here the evidence of "signs and wonders" that the Jews were often asking of Jesus, that they might believe in Him. He had spoken of the Temple as "My Father's house"; He threw out the money changers and traders, reminding them of Old Testament prophecy—"Zeal for your house will consume me"— and so they asked Him, "What sign do you show us for doing these things?" (Psalm 69:9; John 2:18).

Jesus is the Messiah

The healing of the Ruler's son, (4:45-54) was John's second "sign" to 'prove' to his readers that Jesus is the Messiah. And as with the first "sign", water into wine, there is no subsequent teaching immediately following the incident, to help us understand what inferences we can draw from the detail. Two facts are obvious;

- Jesus can 'heal at distance'; He does not 'have to be there', and
- He is not restricted by time.

This latter is particularly brought out in the penultimate, "sign", The Raising of Lazarus. It was not appreciated by Martha, who, when speaking of Lazarus who had been four days in the tomb when Jesus eventually arrived in Bethany, said, "Lord, *if you had been here*, my brother would not have died" (11:21).

The Father's Faith

A noticeable feature in John's account here is the "faith" of the Official. Here was a man who was prepared to believe the word of Jesus and return home, some twenty-five miles, with nothing but a promise.

When the Lord said to him, "Go, your son will live", there was no argument from the man, he straight-way left to go back to his son, because, "*the man believed* the word that Jesus spoke to him".

And later, when it was ascertained that the healing of the boy began at the very hour when Jesus had said, "Your son will live, *he himself believed, and all his household*".

This man's faith is recorded by John as his "second sign"; it is an example of one *who did believe*, and must be seen in the context of John's reason for writing his Gospel, "that you may believe" (20:31).

He stands in sharp contrast to the Jews who demanded of Jesus "signs and wonders" before they would believe (4:48). This man *"believed the word that Jesus spoke to him"* and his faith was rewarded—life for his son. And it eventually led to his whole household believing.

It is interesting to note that the Lord did not say to the Official, 'Your son will be healed', but "Your son lives", (4:50,53 *KJV*); it was not a matter of just getting better but a 'life and death' scenario.

The Greatest Sign

Between these two "signs" we have the Lord's cleansing of the Temple during the Passover in Jerusalem, where the Jews ask for a "sign" of His authority to do this. His reply was, "Destroy this temple, and in three days I will raise it up."

Thinking that He was referring to the Temple that had so far been forty-six years in the building, they said (probably in derision) "and will you raise it up in three days?" But He was referring to the raising of "the temple of his body", a 'figure' that even His disciples did not understand until after His resurrection (2:13-22). This was the greatest "sign" of all.

In Matthew 12:38-40, on being asked for a "sign" by some scribes and Pharisees, Jesus promised that "evil and adulterous generation" that it (his resurrection) would be the only "sign" He would give them, saying, "As Jonah was three days and three nights in the belly of the great fish, so will the Son of Man be three days and three nights in the heart of the earth".

John's Gospel and the world

In John's Gospel, and before he narrates a third sign, John records two important conversations. In chapter 3 Nicodemus is taught: "You must be born again" (3-8), and this culminates in the statement that:

> "**God so loved the world**, that he gave his only Son, that whosoever believes in him should not perish but have eternal life." (3:16)

And in chapter 4 Jesus reveals Himself to the Samaritan woman as the Messiah, leading to the testimony of the Samaritans with whom He stayed two days:

> "This is indeed **the Saviour of the world**." (4:25,26,42; cp. 1:29)

So, sandwiched between the first two "signs", we are reminded that whilst John wrote his Gospel initially to his own people to the intent that they might believe that Jesus is the Messiah, the Son of God, that was not the *ultimate* 'goal' of his record.

Underlying Israel's acceptance of Jesus as the Messiah was *a world-wide purpose* that was to be ministered to "all peoples." Promised to Abraham and his seed (Genesis 12:1-3) it was to be brought about through a nation being "born again" and ministered by them to bring world-wide blessing to all nations—"Salvation is from the Jews" (4:22) .

Jesus the Messiah was "the Lamb of God who takes away *the sin of the world*", (John 1:29).

7. The Invalid: Thirty-eight years

Immediately following the second "sign" John records the visit of Jesus to Jerusalem, where amongst the many "blind, lame and paralysed" people lying around a pool called Bethesda, He noticed one man in particular; one who had been an invalid for thirty-eight years. And it was the Sabbath (5:1-17). Like others, the man believed that if someone would put him in this pool when its "water is stirred up" (possibly by the action of an intermittent spring), he would be healed; but there was no one to help him. The Lord asked the man, "Do you want to be healed?" and following the man's explanation of his predicament, said, "Get up, take up your bed and walk." The effect was immediate, "at once the man was healed and he took up his bed and walked". But instead of rejoicing with him and marvelling at the miracle, the Jews said to the man who had been healed, "*It is the Sabbath*, and it is not lawful for you to take up your bed" (v.9).

This is John's first reference to the Sabbath, and it introduces a long conversation between Jesus and the Jews where His authority and "equality with God" are called into question. John tells us:

> This was why the Jews were persecuting Jesus, because he was doing these things (miracles) on the Sabbath ... not only was he *breaking the Sabbath*, he was even calling God his own Father, *making himself equal with God*. (5:16-18)

The third sign

This third "sign", the healing of the invalid at the pool of Bethesda, demonstrates the wider reason why the Jews were rejecting Jesus, and is an expansion of John's statement in 1:11: "He came to his own (world) and *his own* (*people*) *did not receive him*".

They were unable to enter the pool of healing in their own strength, but rejected the One who could heal them.

It calls to mind the Lord's lament over Jerusalem as recorded by Luke and which underlies Paul's heartfelt prayer Romans 9:1-3, where he is in anguish for his brethren who were rejecting the Messiah.

Luke records the Lord words:

> "O Jerusalem, Jerusalem, the city that kills the prophets and stones those who are sent to it! *How often would I have gathered your children* together as a hen gathers her brood under her wings, *and you would not.*" (Luke 13:34)

And later, following His triumphal entry into Jerusalem when He saw the city, He wept saying,

> "What that you, even you, had known on this day the things that make for peace! But now they are hidden from your eyes" (Luke 19:41,42).

Looked at from one point of view, the Gospel records are histories of the rejection by the Jewish nation of Jesus as Messiah, but with an appendix of hope occasioned by His resurrection. One commentator actually refers to some who see John's Gospel as "The Gospel of the rejection" (R.V.G. Tasker Tyndale *Commentaries*).

The Acts of the Apostles, resting on the resurrected Messiah, is the record of Israel's 'second chance'; an opportunity to which, as a nation, they did not respond. John and Paul wrote whilst that 'chance' remained, both witnessing to Jesus in their writings and referring the Jews to their own prophetic Scriptures—"Jesus is the Messiah, the Son of God" (John 20:30,31; Acts 9:20-22; cp.14:8-10).

The Thirty-eight years

The Lord was called to account both for the healing of the invalid man (5:16) and the blind man (9:14-16), and the problem was, He performed these miracles *on the Sabbath*. The former was carrying his bed in violation of the Law, and as Jeremiah 17:22 recalled:

> Do not bear a burden on the Sabbath day … or do any work, but keep the Sabbath day holy, as I commanded your fathers.

This "sign" is "the first open declaration of hostility to Christ" (Westcott *in loco*). And in 5:16, John records that:

> This was why the Jews were persecuting Jesus, because *he was doing these things.*

Wescott has, "*used to do*, was *in the habit of* doing these things." This was no isolated incident but why did John pick this particular "sign" to try and convince his readers that Jesus is the

Messiah?

The invalid had been in his condition *for 38 years*, and maybe John expected his readers to notice that this was the length of time that the LORD punished the Moses' generation in the wilderness (40 minus 2, cp. Numbers 1:1). And that generation through unbelief refused to go into The Promised Land, into their promised "rest".

The writer of Hebrews used this failure of the Moses' generation as an example to warn his own generation of doing something similar. They could also fail to enter into that "rest ("a *Sabbath rest*" 4:9) due to unbelief. Having cited Psalm 95:7-11, that relates the failure of the Moses' generation, the writer went on:

> Therefore, while the promise of entering (God's) rest *still stands*, let us fear lest any of you should seem to have failed to reach it. (Hebrews 3:7-4:1)

Writing during the Acts period, both John and the writer of Hebrews spoke of the situation that existed at that time. There was still the opportunity and hope for Israel to enter into their "Sabbath rest". And this continued to be so as late as Acts 28, when Paul reminded the Jewish leaders:

> "It is because of *the hope of Israel* that I am wearing this chain" (Acts 28:20).

That "hope" he had earlier expressed as "my hope in the promise made by God to our fathers, to which *our twelve tribes* hope to attain" (26:6,7). He looked forward in "hope" to his own generation of Jews, settled tribe by tribe in The Promised Land (see Ezekiel 47:13-48:29).

As a Jew and an apostle to the circumcision (Galatians 2:7-9), John had the same "hope" as Paul had at that time, and was just as concerned as the Hebrews writer that his people, like the Moses generation, would fail to enter God's Sabbath rest. And like the invalid of 38 years who needed Jesus, John urges his readers to believe that Jesus is the Messiah, the Son of God and have new life in His name (John 20:30-31) .

8. The Feeding of the 5000

This fourth "sign" is probably the best known of the "signs" recorded in John's Gospel (John 6:1-15; 22-59; (if unfamiliar with this miracle please read these passages before continuing with this chapter).

It is also recorded by all three Synoptists (Matthew 14:13-21; Mark 6:30-44; Luke 9:10-17). It is one of only two miracles recorded by John that appear in the Gospels of the other Evangelists; the other is the fifth "sign", Walking on the water.

This latter "sign" splits John's record of the feeding of the 5,000 into two parts; 6:1-15 relates the actual miracle, and 6:22-59 records the Lord's teaching based upon the miracle. Hence, we have (see structure of all the signs at the beginning of this book):

> **Da** The Feeding of 5000—"buy bread that these people
> may eat" (v.5) 6:1-15.
> **E** Walking on the water "It is I, do not be afraid"
> (v.20) 6:16-21.
> **Db** The Feeding of the 5000 "I am the bread of life"
> (v.35) 6:22-59.

Of the great characters in Old Testament times revered by the Jews, John draws attention to two in particular, Abraham and Moses. Others like Jacob, Elijah and David have brief mentions, but these two, with whom the Lord made the two covenants upon which the nation was built, have an important role to play in John's record.

Hence John devotes a long passage (8:33-59) to a conversation that revolves around who are the true seed of Abraham, and Moses is mentioned some 13 times, and that includes the passage before us.

Here we are concerned with Moses, Israel's great Law Giver, who is mentioned in John's Gospel on nine separate occasions. This is a significant fact to take into account when considering for whom John originally wrote it and when. Briefly listed they are:

1	1:17	The law was given through *Moses*; grace and truth came through Jesus Christ.
2	1:45	Philip to Nathaniel, "We have found him of whom *Moses* in the law wrote … Jesus Christ".
3	3:14	As *Moses* lifted up the serpent in the wilderness, so must the Son of Man be lifted up...
4	5:45,46	Jesus to the Jews, "There is one who accuses you: *Moses* on whom you have set your hope".
5	6:32	Jesus to the crowd, "It was not *Moses* who gave you the bread from heaven, but my Father …The bread of God is he who comes down from heaven".
6	7:19	Jesus to the Jews, "Has not *Moses* given you the law? Yet none of you keeps the law".
7	7:22,23	"You circumcise on the Sabbath … so that the law of *Moses* may not be broken (yet) you are angry with me because on the Sabbath I made a man whole".
8	8:5	Woman caught in adultery: Scribes and Pharisees to Jesus, "in the Law *Moses* commanded us to stone such women. So what do you say?" … "Let the sinless one cast the first stone".
9	9:28,29	The Jews to the healed blind man, "You are His (Jesus) disciple, but we are disciples of *Moses*".

Who has the final authority?

Underlying all these references is the question of who has the final 'authority'? Moses was the Jews final authority, they were his disciples, but Jesus accuses them of 'not keeping Moses' law'. And it was Moses who pointed forward to the Promised One who would come, contrasting the "grace" that was inherent in the Law with the "true grace" that came through Jesus Christ—"grace for grace".

Note that "Grace and (*kai*) truth" in John 1:14 may be a figure of speech where two things are put for one, hence "true grace").

It would be wrong to think that the giving of the Law through Moses was not an act of grace towards His people, but Jesus the Messiah came "full of true grace" and "to fulfil the law" (Matthew 5:17).

The Old Testament history is full of 'type' that foreshadows the 'anti-type' seen in the New Testament, and with this fourth "sign", "manna (bread) from heaven", foreshadowed the feeding of the 5000. The bread that sustained life in the wilderness was a 'type' of "the bread of God who comes down from heaven"— Jesus the Messiah (6:32,33). Moses, speaking to his generation said:

> "The LORD your God will raise up for you *a prophet like me* from among you … it is to him you shall listen … whosoever will not listen to my words that he shall speak in my name, I myself will require it of him." (Deuteronomy 18:15,19)

Peter identified "The Prophet" as one and the same as the

Messiah when he quoted the Deuteronomy passage to the Jews in Acts 3:22,23, but this was not apparently generally believed by the Jews at this time (cp. John 1:19-21; 7:40). After the Feeding of the 5000, the people who had seen this "sign" said, "This is indeed *the* Prophet who is to come into the world" John 6:14). As Lightfoot noted:

> The connection is not obvious, and the writer has not explained himself. The missing link is supplied by t*he Messianic conception of the age* (my italics). The prophet foretold was to be like Moses himself. Hence it was inferred that there must be a parallel in the works of the two. Hence a repetition of the gift of the manna—the bread from heaven—might be expected. Was not this miracle then the very fulfilment of their expectation?

The Prophet

So "the next day", and with the miraculous feeding of the 5000 fresh in their minds, the crowd sought Jesus out to confirm in their minds their earlier assessment of who He was—"this is indeed the Prophet who is to come into the world".

He had withdrawn overnight from them when they attempted to "take him by force and make him king" (6:14,15), now they were apparently having second thoughts.

They asked Him for another "sign" and said, "What work do you perform?", citing Moses and the giving of manna from heaven as a work of God. It may be that just as the Moses' generation actually *saw* the manna descend from heaven, so they were looking for such a sign from Jesus.

Another sign!

This demand for another "sign" preceded the long discourse on 'the true bread from heaven'. Failing to understand its significance, some of His disciples deserted Him, leaving mainly only the Twelve who stood by Him (6:35-71). The essence of this teaching is,

> "I am the bread of life, whoever comes to me shall not hunger, and whoever believes in me shall never thirst" (6:35).

Of the "signs" that John selects to convince his brethren that "Jesus is the Messiah, the Son of God", The Feeding of the 5000 is perhaps the one, more than all the other "signs", that should provide 'proof' that this is true.

Its connection to Moses and the history of Israel in the wilderness, in particular the "manna from heaven", and the initial reaction of those who saw it, should strike a chord with Jewish expectations—"This is indeed the Prophet who is to come into the world" (6:14).

So why did the nation not respond to it. That is another story! (See the author's *Paul's Letter to the Romans: Background and Introduction* for more on this.)

9. Walking on the Water

The expression, 'walking on water' is used sarcastically in modern parlance of someone who ostensibly claims to have done, or claims to be able to do, something physically impossible. In John 6:16-21 it is a "sign" related by John to demonstrate the Messiahship of Jesus of Nazareth. It is placed between the two sections of The Feeding of the 5000 (the actual feeding) and the Lord's teaching that sprang from it.

This incident is also recorded by Matthew (14:22-33) and Mark (6:45-52). Matthew's account adds the attempt by Peter to walk on the water and his faith failing him (14:28-31), and also when they were all safely in the boat, the worship of the disciples saying to Jesus, "Truly you are the Son of God" (33), both omitted by Mark and John.

It would be foolish not to admit that there are difficulties in trying to synchronise the three accounts of this miracle. For one thing, the words in John 6:19, *epi tes thalasses* "on the sea" (*KJV*) have been understood by some to mean "on the seashore" as in John 21:1 ("at" or "by" the sea). If this is so then there is no miracle (or "sign") here at all!

That this is not so, however, is clear as the disciples are said to have been, "in the midst of the sea" (Mark 6:47 lit.) when they met Jesus. So this is, indeed, a fifth "sign" whether John refers to it as such or not, and as Matthew records of this One whom "the winds and sea obey", the disciples identified Him as "the Son of God" (8:27; 14:33).

What lead to this sign?

One of the important facts to notice about this fifth "sign" is what led to it in the first place. The people who witnessed 'The feeding of the 5000', said of Jesus,

> "This is indeed the Prophet who is to come into the world", attempted to "take him by force to make him king." (John 6:14,15).

But He was having none of this, and as at other times He withdrew to be by Himself, no doubt because His time had not yet come (cp. 2:4). The events in the life of Jesus on earth did not happen haphazardly, but proceeded in such a way that "in the fullness of time" God's purpose in sending His Son would be achieved (Galatians 4:4,5). Any other 'Messiah', (and there had been many beforehand and there would be plenty to come), would have accepted the peoples' adulation and become their king.

Some have looked for some indication in Old Testament prophecy of the walking on the water by the Son of God. Suggestions are Job 9:8 where, in his reply to Bildad the Shuhite, Job said of God, who *"trampled the waves of the sea"*. Or perhaps more obviously, where the Psalmist "ponders the work of God":

> When the waters saw you, O God, when the waters saw you, they were afraid; indeed the deep trembled … Your way was *through the sea*, your path *through the great waters*; yet *your footprints* were unseen. (Psalm 77:12,16,19)

> "The Evangelist (John) was describing an event in which he saw Jesus as the revelation of God coming to his

disciples in their distress—*in the second exodus*" G.R. Beasley-Murray *in loco* (*Word Biblical Commentary*).

The 'I Am' statements

The Gospel of John is well known for the various "I Am's" (*ego eimi*) that Jesus claimed to be. And in each case, they reflect an aspect of the Messiah, the Son of God, and summarize his role in revelation and salvation.

He said "I am" ...

- The bread of life (6:35) the true bread from heaven in contrast to the manna in Moses' day (6:32).
- The light of the world (8:12) the true light that came into the world (1:9; 9:5).
- The door of the sheep (10:7) protecting the sheep in the sheepfold and the only entrance to salvation (10:9).
- The good shepherd (10:14) who lays down His life for the sheep (10:11).
- The resurrection and the life (11:25) for the believer who, "though he die, yet shall he live".
- The true and living way (14:6) the only way to the Father.
- The true vine (15:1) of which believers are the branches who "can do nothing" unless they abide in Him (15:5).

One occurrence of *ego eimi* that is not obvious in many English versions occurs in this fifth "sign" in John 6:20.

When Jesus was walking on the sea He approached the boat which the disciples were struggling to control in a strong wind and a rough sea. They saw Him coming near to the boat and were frightened. Matthew's version says they thought it was a ghost. But He assures them, "It is I; do not be afraid".

"It is I" is the translation of *ego eimi*, literally, "I am". *Young's Literal Version* actually translates, "I am *he. Be not afraid*". (On a lower plane, a modern example of this situation might be if a man returns unexpectedly early from work, and as he walks through the door calls to his wife to reassure her, "It's only me.")

The very presence of Jesus was all the assurance the disciples needed, and "they were glad to take him into the boat" (John 6:19-21). A lesson for all generations of believers in whatever calling.

The Divine Name

Beasley-Murray says of the usage of the expression *ego eimi* here, and particularly in 8:24,28,58 and 13;19, "indicates a unique relationship to God, recalling the divine name in Exodus 3:14 and the affirmations of Isaiah (e.g.):

> "You are my witnesses", declares the LORD, "and my servant whom I have chosen, that you may know and believe me and understand that I am (Septuagint *ego eimi*) he ... I am the LORD, and besides me is no saviour". (Isaiah 43:10,11)

Anyone reading the Greek version of the Old Testament (Septuagint *LXX*), the version most in use in New Testament times, might see an obvious parallel between God's name given to Moses, Isaiah's prophecy and the Lord's words to His disciples:

Exodus 3:14 *LXX* And God spoke to Moses, saying, *"ego eimi ho On* (I am THE BEING)" ...

- Isaiah 43:10 *LXX* "You are my witnesses declares the LORD ... *ego eimi* (I am) he".
- John 6:20 *ESV* Jesus said to the disciples, *"ego eimi me phobeisthe* (It is I; do not be afraid"). *Young's Literal Version,* "I am *he. Be not afraid."*

What the Jews understood by the claims of Jesus are clearly seen in their reactions to Him. He was not only "breaking the Sabbath, but he was even *calling God his own Father, making himself equal (isos) with God"* (5:18).

And the Jews' reaction both here and later, when He said to them, "Before Abraham was, I am", was to seek to kill Him. Much later Paul was to write of Jesus, He "did not count *equality (isos)* with God a thing to be grasped", (Philippians 2:7).[1]

---

[1] For more on this subject see *The I AM Statements of Jesus* by W M Henry, published by The Open Bible Trust.

10. The Man Born Blind

This is the second "sign" in which a connection between disability and "sin" is made. In the earlier (third) "sign", a man who had been an invalid for 38 years was told by Jesus after he had been healed, "See, you are well! *Sin no more*, that nothing worse may happen to you" (5:14).

Here, in the sixth "sign", when Jesus' disciples see the blind man they say to Him, "Rabbi, *who sinned*, this man or his parents, that he was born blind?". But the Lord's reply was, "It was not that this man sinned, or his parents, but that the works of God might be displayed in him" (9:1-3).

The idea that the man's parents might be responsible takes us back to the Second Commandment, which speaks of "visiting the iniquity of the fathers on the children" and which occasioned the proverb, "The fathers have eaten sour grapes, and the children's teeth are set on edge", (Exodus 20:5; Jeremiah 31:29). (For more on this see the author's *The Ten Commandments* OBT).

This man had been "blind from birth ... *to let the work of God be illustrated in him*" (*Moffatt*). This calls to mind what Jesus was later to say of Lazarus, "This illness does not lead to death. *It is for the glory of God, so that the Son of God may be glorified through it*" (11:4). (Keep in mind that in both cases the "illness" was 'cured' by Jesus.) All that Jesus did had, as its goal, the manifestation of "the work of God" and His glory.

A difficult question

Are we to believe that this poor man had to suffer blindness for many years *in order to* display the work of God? This thought is difficult to gainsay.

In the wider picture it is reminiscent of that enigma that has faced mankind from ages past to the present day—'Why do the innocent suffer?' Job and his companions struggled with it (See the author's *The Book of Job: Suffering and the Deep Things of God*), and in modern times so did C.S. Lewis (*The Problem of Pain*) and many others. I don't have an answer to it, and am driven back to Paul's observation in Romans 9:14-24 on the sovereignty of God—"Is there injustice on God's part? By no means! ... Will what is moulded say to its moulder, '*Why have you made me like this?*'" Is this what the blind man wondered?

What we can say, however, is that this man's physical condition and his words after his recovery, are not simply a "sign" or a "work of God" recorded by John to show that Jesus is the Messiah, but that it is a "sign" for all time. Christians can truly say, "One thing I do know, that though I was blind, now I see" (9:25). With his sight restored, one would think that this man's troubles were now over, but not so. Instead of rejoicing with him that he could now see, he is put under pressure from all sides. Some of his neighbours doubt initially that he is the same man "who used to sit and beg". Then they question him about Jesus; "Where is he?" And they ask, "how were your eyes opened?" (9:8-12).

He is interrogated twice by the Pharisees (13-17; 24-34), who even involve his parents in their interrogation (18-23). And finally, when the man becomes bold, and expresses his amazement that the Pharisees "do not know where (Jesus) comes from and yet he opened my eyes", they "cast him out" (v.34).

Cast out

In Jerusalem at this time there were two smaller courts or Synagogue Councils (Westcott), and the interrogation by the Pharisees probably took place in one of these. So, the "casting out" may simply mean that the man was thrown out of here.

At this point in time, the man had only referred to the Lord as, "The man called Jesus" and "a prophet" (vs.11,17). It was only later after Jesus heard that he had been cast out, and found him, that he acknowledged Jesus as "the Son of God" and worshipped Him (vs. 35-38 *KJV*).

So, since "the Jews had already agreed that if anyone should confess Jesus to be Messiah, he was to be put out of the Synagogue" (9:22; cp. 12:42), it is probable that he did end up excommunicated, excluding him from all religious fellowship, from "the congregation of Israel" (cp. Matthew 18:17).

This exclusion from the Synagogue was what the Lord warned His disciples would happen to them if they bore witness to Him (16:2). And John, although he wrote his gospel with the object that his readers might believe that Jesus is the Messiah (20:30,31), does not hold back the possible consequences of doing so.

Apart from the obvious fact that this "sign" shows that Jesus is the long-awaited Messiah as prophesied, who gives sight to the blind (Luke 4:18; 7:18-22), there is an obvious play on the concept of 'blindness' in the consequent teaching of Jesus:

> "For judgement I came into this world, that those who do not see may see, and those who see may become blind". Some of the Pharisees near him heard these things, and

said to him, "Are we also blind?" Jesus said to them, "If you were blind you would have no guilt, but now that you say, 'We see', your guilt remains". (9:39-41)

Luke 10:21 is a commentary on these verses. Jesus, "in the same hour" that the seventy-two disciples returned from their highly successful mission, rejoiced in the Holy Spirit and said, "I thank you, Father, Lord of heaven and earth, that you have hidden these things from the wise and understanding and revealed them to little children."

In John 9, "those who do not see" look back to the blind man, 'kept in the dark' from birth, but who through the ministration of the Lord is able to say, "now I see". He is a type of the many who have "no intellectual knowledge, no clear perception of the divine will and the divine law" (Westcott), represented in Luke's account by "little children." It is to them that the "things" of God are revealed.

"Those who see", or perhaps "Claim to see" (John 9:41) are represented in John's account by the Pharisees, who ask (sarcastically) "Are we also blind?" To them these "things" were hidden. Paul referring to many of the Jews at that time, named them as those who "claim to see" in Romans 2:17-20:

> You call yourself a Jew and rely on the law and boast in God and know his will and approve what is excellent, because you are instructed from the law; and you are sure that you yourself are a guide to the blind, a light to those who are in darkness, an instructor of the foolish.

And Paul goes on to show the utter 'hypocrisy' of these men who don't 'practice what they preach', a word the Lord used many times of their ilk (eight times in Matthew 23 alone). They should have been "a light to those in darkness" (cp. Acts 13:47), but instead, "the name of God is blasphemed among the Gentiles because of you", (Romans 2:24). Thankfully, the healing of the blind man stands out as an example of what "the work of God" can do, and thankfully Christians today can say, "now I see".

11. The Raising of Lazarus

This last "sign" pre-resurrection (11:1-44), has so many salient points. Initially I shall look at the narrative that leads up to the actual miracle, and afterwards consider the "sign" itself and its outcome. (The narrative is very detailed, so if unfamiliar with it, please read.)

This seventh "sign" demonstrates:

> The immeasurable greatness of (God's) power towards us who believe, according to the working of *his great might that he worked in Christ when he raised him from the dead* and seated him at his right hand in the heavenly places, far above all … (Ephesians 2:19-21)

This 'rising from the dead' was the ultimate miracle, the ultimate "sign" that Jesus is the Messiah; a miracle that reaches out beyond that event in Bethany over 1900 years ago.

The "power" that raised Lazarus from the dead, and raised Christ from the dead and seated Him at the right hand of God, is a "power" that Paul prays we in the Church which is the Body of Christ might "know", for it is "toward us who believe", (Ephesians 1:19-23).

And it is the 'hope' of all God's people for, "If Christ has not been raised, our preaching is in vain and your faith is in vain … you are still in your sins (1 Corinthians 15:14,17).

Other Resurrections

In the other Gospels, two further examples are recorded of Jesus raising someone from the dead; the widow's son at Nain (Luke 7:11-17) and Jairus' daughter (Luke 8:40-42; 49-56).

And when John the Baptist sent his disciples to ask Jesus, "Are you the one who is to come, or shall we look for another?", He sent them back with the message that demonstrated that He was indeed the Messiah saying, "the blind receive their sight and the lame walk, lepers are cleansed and the deaf hear, and *the dead are raised up ..."* (Matthew 11:2-6).

The language used in the last clause, "the dead are raised up" is not dissimilar to Isaiah 26:19, "Your dead shall live; their bodies shall rise. You who dwell in the dust, awake and sing for joy".

This is a passage that is linked to the promise that "the LORD is coming" and that there will be a future judgement on "the inhabitants of the earth" (v.21). This is the age that was anticipated during the Gospel and Acts periods, and about which Hebrews told its readers that they had "tasted the powers of the age to come", (Hebrews 6:4,5).

The Seventh Sign

The Lord and His disciples were empowered to heal the sick and even raise the dead (Matthew 10:8). All these were Messianic "signs". The raising of Lazarus was one of them. (More on this later.)

This seventh "sign" occurred late in the Lord's earthly ministry, when the hostile reaction of the authorities towards Him was intensifying as He went towards Jerusalem for the final time. Hence, the disciples tried to dissuade Him from going to Bethany, only two miles from the great city, because the Jews were seeking to stone Him, but in an enigmatic reply He said, "If anyone walks in the day, he does not stumble". His time had not yet come and no harm would come to Him while it was "the day" (John 11: 9,10).

The Reason for the Delay

Jesus was in no hurry to get to Bethany, which, seen from a human point of view is somewhat disturbing, especially in view of His closeness to the family of Lazarus (11:5). His 'reason' for the delay appears to be partly explained in verses 14,15 lit:

> Then **therefore** (*tote oun*) Jesus told them (the disciples) plainly, 'Lazarus is dead. *For your sake I am glad that I was not there*, so that you may believe'."

The word 'therefore' (omitted from many translations, the *NIV* has "So then") links the Lord's 'delay' to inducing 'the disciples' belief', because they "had failed to catch the meaning of the words with which He had tried their spiritual discernment", (Wescott *in loco*).

Firstly, the disciples appeared not to have appreciated that the illness of Lazarus was "for the glory of God, so that the Son of God may be glorified through it" (11:4). The underlying motive, according to John, of all Jesus' miracles was the glory of God ... the glorification of the Messiah by displaying "the works of God" (9:3; 11:4). And after the departure of Jesus, the Holy Spirit would continue these works through Jesus' disciples and glorify Him as the Messiah (John 16:14).

Secondly, they misunderstood the Lord's reference to Lazarus' death as "sleep", believing that "if he has fallen asleep, he will recover" (vs.11,12). The image of 'sleep' for death is common in Rabbinic writings (Westcott) and it is used elsewhere in Scripture of Stephen and David (Acts 7:60; 13:36) and of Christians who had died during the Acts period (1 Thessalonians 4:13).

Thirdly, the disciples had tried to dissuade the Lord from going to Bethany at all, fearing the Jews who were already seeking His life. But His enigmatic answer (above), concerning the safety of anyone who "walks in the day and who does not stumble", demonstrated His conviction that He was immune from danger as long as there was His Father's work to complete (11:8-10). His time would come, but it was not yet.

Two Great Truths

Together with the "sign" of the healing of the Man born Blind, this "sign" brings out the two great truths concerning Jesus; He is "the light of the world" (9:5) and "the resurrection and the life" (11:25). They come together in the Prologue where John observed, "In him was *life*, and *the life* was *the light* of men" (1:4). But the sad truth was:

> He was in the world, and the world was made through him, yet the world did not know him. He came to his own (world), and his own (people) did not receive him.

He came into the world that **He made**, to a people **to whom He had committed** a worldwide mission to all nations. But when John wrote his Gospel they were rejecting Him as their Messiah, the One through whom alone that purpose could be fulfilled.

John, writing initially to his own people as an apostle to the circumcision (Galatians 2:9) presents his seven (eight) "signs" in order that they might believe that "He is the Messiah, the Son of God", (20:30,31).

And yet: To all who did receive him, who believed in his name, he gave the right to become children (*tekna*) of God, who were born, not of blood nor of the will of the flesh nor of the will of man, but of God. (1:11-13)

Mary and Martha

We now take up the story where the Lord arrives at the home of Martha and Mary, to find that Lazarus was already in the tomb.

I have heard sermons on the Martha/Mary scenario in which Mary is praised above Martha, mainly because she "anointed the Lord with ointment and wiped his feet with her hair", and the Lord had said of her, in contrast to Martha who was "distracted with much serving", "Mary has chosen the good portion" (John 11:2; 12:1-8; cp. Luke 10:38-42). But in the "sign", The Raising of Lazarus, the balance is restored.

"When Martha heard that Jesus was coming, *she went out and met him*, but Mary remained seated in the house", (11:20). On meeting Him she said, "Lord, if you had been here my brother would not have died"; the very same words that Mary used later on meeting Jesus. But the difference between them was that Martha went on to say, "But *even now* I know that whatever you ask from God, God will give you" (John 11:20-22,32,33).

Even Now

Those two words, "even now", may only reveal a glimmer of hope, but what follows shows that Martha, based on what she had learned of Jesus' ministry up till then, exhibited a faith that was to come into full bloom a few verses later when the Lord said to her:

> I am the resurrection and the life. Whoever believes in me, though he die, yet shall he live, and everyone who lives and believes in me shall never die. Do you believe this?

And Martha's answer is the very reason John wrote his Gospel with its "signs" in the first place:

> "Yes Lord; I believe that *you are the Messiah, the Son of God*, who is coming into the world." (v.27)

But when Jesus asked that the stone be removed from Lazarus' tomb, Martha, described now as "the sister of the dead man", said, "Lord, by this time there will be an odour, for he has been dead four days".

Her relationship to her brother made her shrink from looking on the ravages of death of one who was so close to her. Jesus reminds her that if she believed she would see the glory of God. And lifting His eyes up to the Father, the Lord gave thanks that He has heard Him. This He does "on account of the people standing round, that they may believe that the Father had sent Him." And then comes that loud cry from the Lord: "**Lazarus, come out**, and the man who had died came out" (38-44).

Two Effects

This "sign" had two effects upon the Jews; those who had witnessed the miracle "believed in him", but others went and told the Pharisees what Jesus had done, and that led to the chief priests' determination to arrest and kill … not only Jesus, but also the living example of His power, Lazarus (11:46-53; 12:9,10).

The raising of Lazarus may be set alongside those other two well-known miracles where the Lord raised the dead; the widow's son at Nain (Luke 7:11-17) and Jairus' daughter (Luke 8:40-42; 49-56). But whereas an unbeliever might argue that in these latter cases the son and daughter were not really dead, that cannot be said of Lazarus who had been 'dead **and** buried' for four days.

Many Raised

We might also recall that rarely referred to passage which records that:

> The earth shook, and the rocks were split. The tombs were opened. And many bodies of the saints (lit. 'holy ones') who had fallen asleep were raised, and coming out of the tombs after (the Messiah's) resurrection they went into the holy city and appeared to many. (Matthew 27:51-53 *ESV*)

This "bodies of the saints" may conjure up pictures of zombie-like characters wandering around Jerusalem. (There is nothing in this passage to suggest that it was the New Jerusalem!)

Numerous questions come to mind such as, 'What bodies did they have?': 'Where did they go after their appearance in Jerusalem?': 'Why did only Matthew record this spectacular event and how did other Jews, especially the Pharisees, react to their presence?'

Fact or Fiction?

Much has been written on this passage, some of which question whether or not this was an historical event at all, or just "a piece of realised and historicized apocalyptic depending on O.T. Motifs found in such passages as Isaiah 26:9 … and especially (the valley of dry bones) Ezekiel 37:12-14" (e.g. D.A. Hagner in *Word Biblical Commentary*).

I will not burden the reader with all the arguments but simply give my own views. If the events that Matthew has recorded elsewhere in his Gospel are historical, I see no reason why this should not be an historical fact also. And if Lazarus came back from the dead to continue his life as a normal human being on earth, so might these. They would then, like Lazarus, live out what was left of their lives and die just like other people, with the common Jewish 'hope' in a "resurrection on the last day" (John 11:24).

Before or After?

One problem that has concerned many is the alternative way Matthew 27:52,53 may be read. For example, the *NIV* reads:

The earth shook and the rocks split. The tombs broke open and the bodies of many holy people who had died were raised to life. They came out of the tombs, and after Jesus' resurrection they went into the holy city and appeared to many people.

This suggests that they were raised from the dead *before* the resurrection of Christ, and at the same time as the earthquake, the very moment of the death of Christ. Hence, some question how could Jesus be the first to rise from the dead, as Paul stated in Acts 26:23? But then, the same problem arises with Lazarus, and those others who rose from the dead during the Gospel period.

It is evident that Paul, who himself had brought back to life the young man Eutychus who had fallen from the third storey of the building where he was preaching (Acts 20:7-12), did not look upon 'resurrections' such as that of Lazarus in the same light as that of Jesus.

Christ's resurrection was the greatest "sign" of all that showed He was the Messiah, the Son of God. He **was** "The resurrection and the Life". This we must look at in the next chapter.

12. Christ's Resurrection

The Sign of the Prophet Jonah

This is not a chapter on the resurrection of the Messiah *per se*, but mainly of that event seen as a "sign" that He is the Messiah, the Son of God, "in accordance with the Scriptures", and particularly here the Old Testament prophecy of Jonah.

Strange as it may seem, references to "the sign of the prophet Jonah" do not occur in John's Gospel where Jesus is presented as filling this role. Only Matthew (12:38-42; 16:4) and Luke (11:29-32), compare the experience of Jesus with that of Jonah.

John does, however, recall that Jesus early in His ministry had said, "Destroy this temple, and in three days I will raise it up", speaking of "the temple of his body", an enigma that none, not even His disciples, understood until after He was raised from the dead (2:18-22). The Jews had asked for a "sign" (v.18), and this would be it.

The Greatest Sign

The resurrection of Jesus is the greatest "sign" of all, demonstrating that He is "both Lord and Messiah" (Acts 2:32-36), and for the disbelieving scribes and Pharisees it was the only "sign" that God would give them. When they asked of Jesus a "sign" He answered:

> "An evil and adulterous generation seeks for a sign, but no sign will be given to it except the sign of the prophet Jonah. For just as Jonah was three days and three nights in

the belly of the great fish, so will the Son of Man be three days and three nights in the heart of the earth." (Matthew 12:38-40)

The full meaning of these words would not of course be understood except in retrospect, but even after the resurrection many of the Jewish authorities were not only unconvinced, but actively went about to deny it.

Firstly they "secured the tomb" against His disciples removing the body and faking His resurrection, and then when that failed, bribing the guard to say that "His disciples came by night and stole him away while we were asleep" (Matthew 28:62-66, 11-15).

But it could not be denied, for within a very short time the Lord's disciples were proclaiming the resurrection of Jesus in Jerusalem, and the rest is history.

Resurrection Morning

John does not actually present the resurrection of the Messiah as a "sign" in the same way that he does for example, when Jesus turned Water into Wine (1:11) or The Healing of the Ruler's Son (4:54), he leaves his readers to deduce it themselves.

He relates the events of the resurrection morning when Mary Magdalene coming to the tomb first, noticed that the stone had been taken away, and that the tomb was empty.

Her first reaction was that someone (possibility the authorities) had "taken the Lord out of the tomb", and she conveyed this to Peter and John (the other disciple) saying, "we do not know where they have laid him". They ran to the tomb and John outran Peter. John looked in first, but Peter actually went into the tomb. They saw the burial cloths lying there and "the other disciple who had reached the tomb first, now went in, and he saw and believed" (v.8).

Believed what?

I do not think that John in recording this of himself, is claiming that he was the first to believe that Jesus had risen from the dead, only that Mary's observation was correct, the tomb **was** empty.

I say this because the next clause shows that at that moment in time none of the disciples had understood the ancient prophecy— "for as yet they did not understand the Scripture, that he must rise from the dead." They then returned to their homes (John 20:1-10).

The ancient prophecy John had in mind was possibly Psalm 16:10: "You will not abandon my soul to Sheol, or let your holy one see corruption", as referred to by Peter on the Day Of Pentecost (Acts 2:29-32).

The story continues; Mary Magdalene first, then the disciples, even 'doubting Thomas', see the Lord and believe—"**He is risen**". The whole of Christendom, past, present and future hangs on this claim as Paul wrote:

> If Christ has not been raised, then our preaching is in vain and your faith is in vain … if Christ has not been raised, your faith is futile and you are still in your sins. (1 Corinthians 15:14,17)

Paul had begun this section of this epistle by setting out "the gospel" that he had "received through a revelation of Jesus Christ" (v.3; Galatians 1:11,12):

> "Christ died for our sins in accordance with the Scriptures, that he was buried, that he was raised on the third day in accordance with the Scriptures, and that he appeared to Cephas (Peter) ... the twelve (apostles) ... then to more than five hundred brethren at one time ... James ... all the apostles ... last of all to me ..." (1 Corinthians 15:3- 8)

Resurrection and the Gospel

This "gospel" he referred to "as of first importance", is outlined here where he wrote reminding the Corinthians, "of the gospel *I preached to you*, which *you received, in which you stand*, and *by which you are being saved ...*"

Although later Paul emphasised that the resurrection is the most essential fact of the "gospel", it is important, just as it was in the case of Lazarus, to note that He was 'dead **and** buried'.

Lazarus had been dead four days when the Lord arrived in Bethany, and was already in the tomb.

Jesus was, like Jonah, "three days and three nights in the heart of the earth." Jonah was the Old Testament type and Lazarus the New Testament type of Jesus in resurrection. In human parlance, "dead and buried" denotes the end of all hope, but not where God is concerned, and Jesus is "the resurrection and the life".

It is gratifying to note that from the earliest times the 'facts' of the Gospel were included in declarations of faith. In *The Book of Common Prayer* used in the Church of England, The Apostles'

Creed affirms—"I believe … in Jesus Christ … *who was crucified, dead, and buried … the third day he rose again from the dead …*". It appears also in the second Article of Religion in that same book.

The Greatest Sign

The resurrection of the Messiah is undoubtedly the greatest of John's "signs". It brings to a climax the seven pre-resurrection "signs" that he picked out from the "many signs that Jesus did in the presence of his disciples" (20:30).

In another place, His resurrection is described by the Lord himself as "the sign of the prophet Jonah", and it was the only "sign" that He said He would give to "an evil and adulterous generation" (Matthew 12:38-40). It was the key thought in Peter's address to his own people on The Day of Pentecost:

> *This Jesus God raised up*, and of that we are all witnesses … Let all the house of Israel therefore know for certain that God has made him both Lord and Messiah, this Jesus whom you crucified. (Acts 2:32,36)

And the facts of the gospel are used elsewhere by Paul, where he teaches the practical outcome of the believer's position in Christ—"in which you stand"—when he speaks of the identification of the believer with Christ in Romans 6:1-6.

Here he writes of being *"buried with him by baptism unto death … united with him in resurrection …"* but later, when we move from the earthly "hope of Israel" to the "hope" of the Church which is the Body of Christ, we are even *"seated with him in the heavenly places"* (Ephesians 2:6; Colossians 2:11-13.). For more on this see the author's *Paul's Letter to the Romans* and *The Mystery of Ephesians* OBT.

13. The Draught of Fish

In the first twenty chapters of his Gospel, John has recorded seven "signs", finishing with the words:

> Now Jesus did many other *signs* in the presence of his disciples, which are not written in this book; but these are written so that you may believe that Jesus is the Messiah, the Son of God, and that by believing you may have life in his name. (20:30,31)

As I pointed out earlier in this book, it is at this point that many commentators consider chapter twenty-one was added on later; by John certainly, and not too long after the 'original' Gospel of twenty chapters was written. This, in my view, does not affect the belief that this, just as much as the rest of the Gospel, is part of the inspired Word of God.

What has been questioned, however, is whether The Draught of Fish recorded in this chapter is an eighth "sign". It could also be questioned whether it was a miracle ("sign") at all, and if so, in what sense? Let us look at the 'facts'.

A miraculous sign or not?

Without going into where the Twelve apostles spent the forty-nine days between Passover and Pentecost (fiftieth), and whether or not some of them returned to their fishing business, there was certainly one occasion during this period, when the Lord "revealed himself again to the disciples by the sea of Tiberius (Galilee)" (John 21:1).

John tells us it was "the third time … after the Lord was raised from the dead". And it was to seven of His disciples (John 21:1-14). Evidently, most, if not all of the Twelve, had remained together, and now when Peter said, "I am going fishing", the seven (some named in v.2) said, "We will go with you". But they had a fruitless night; "they caught nothing."

At this point we must consider whether the following events constitute a miracle, and an eighth "sign". We might note that the word "sign" (*semeion*) does not always refer to a miracle in the New Testament. For example, although we cannot doubt that the birth of the baby Jesus was miraculous, there was nothing miraculous about the "sign" that the angel gave to the shepherds:

> "This will be a sign (*semeion*) for you; you will find a baby wrapped in swaddling clothes and lying in a manger" (Luke 2:12).

Likewise, there is nothing miraculous in "the sign (*semeion*) of circumcision" (Romans 4:11). So, let us apply this to The Draught of Fish. Back to the narrative.

As they approached land, the disciples saw Jesus standing on the shore. He called out to them, "Children, do you have any fish?" They reply, "No".

He now instructs them to, "Cast the net on the right side of the boat", and when they do so, they have a "net full of fish" (153 when counted).

Now the question; was this a miracle, and if so in what sense? Did the Lord 'create' 153 fish for the disciples to catch, or were they there all the time, but not in the particular area where the disciples had been fishing?

Every sea fisherman, and probably most people, will be aware that fish gather in shoals. They do so for security and to increase their chance of successful mating. So that if a net is dragged along one area of the sea it might gather little or nothing, but even a short distance away there may be an abundance of fish for the asking; it is a matter of knowing where. Finding this area might just be a matter of 'luck', or more probably, deduced by experienced fishermen. In the Atlantic for example, it might be revealed by observing where many gulls are wheeling round or where many dolphins are gathering. In the normal course of events, no 'miracle' is involved, unless we take 'knowledge' as a miracle.

Creation or Knowledge?

I have no wish to detract from John's narrative and the inspired Word of God; the Lord, who made all things (John 1:3) could have made 153 fish for the disciples to catch—a miracle of creation.

Or He could be demonstrating His intimate knowledge of the creation by knowing *where* such a shoal of fish was gathered in such abundance at that time.

What cannot be denied is that as a result of the multitude of fish caught, John ("that disciple whom Jesus loved") *"therefore said to Peter*, 'It is the Lord!'" (21:6,7). The great catch of fish revealed, as it did in the other seven "signs", that Jesus is the Son of God. John may not have called it a "sign" or a miracle, but seeing it convinced him that this was the Lord himself, and this is why he recorded this post-resurrection event. This 'knowledge' of Jesus was demonstrated earlier in John's Gospel in the case of Nathanael:

Jesus saw Nathanael coming towards him and said of him, "Behold, an Israelite indeed, in whom there is no deceit!" Nathanael said to him, "How do you know me?" Jesus answered him, "Before Philip called you, when you were under the fig tree. I saw you." Nathanael answered him, "Rabbi, you are the Son of God! You are the King of Israel!" Jesus answered him, "Because I said to you, 'I saw you under the fig tree,' do you believe? You will see greater things than these. Truly, truly I say to you, you will see heaven opened, and the angels of God ascending and descending on the Son of Man. (1:47-51)

There are obviously truths underlying this record of John, not least the comparison of Nathanael with Old Testament Jacob, who had his name changed to 'Israel'—"an Israelite indeed".

And also, the allusion to Jacob's experience when he saw "a ladder set up on earth, and the top of it reached to heaven ... the angels of God were ascending and descending on it!" (Genesis 28:12).

But that is not in the remit of this study. It is enough here to note what Jesus 'saw' and 'knew' of Nathanael that brought out of him that confession, "You are the Son of God! You are the King of Israel!" ('King of Israel' is tantamount to saying, 'Messiah', as Lightfoot showed in *Biblical Essays*, cp. John 1:41 with 1:49).

153 Fish

The significance of the 153 fish has tested the minds of many down the ages and produced some strange and sometimes complicated suggestions.

An early commentary on Ezekiel (474 B.C.) refers to a learned poet Oppianus Cilix who said that there are 153 different species of fish (*Word Biblical Commentary* on John *in loco*).

Others looked for a mathematical solution and *Gematria* (a term derived from geometry) is popular (see E.W. Bullinger's *Number in Scripture* published by Kregel for more on this).

Post Script

However, I would like to close this book by reminding the reader that John summed up his Gospel so:

> Now Jesus did many other *signs* in the presence of his disciples, which are not written in this book; but these are written so that you may believe that Jesus is the Messiah, the Son of God, and that by believing you may have life in his name. (John 20:30,31)

More on the Signs in John's Gospel

That you may believe
(The Eight Signs of John's Gospel)
by Charles Ozane

In this book the author has given careful consideration to each of John's eight miraculous signs.

He shows that each miraculous sign has ...

- A national fulfilment in the future for Israel

as well as ...

- An individual fulfilment in the present for the believer in Christ.

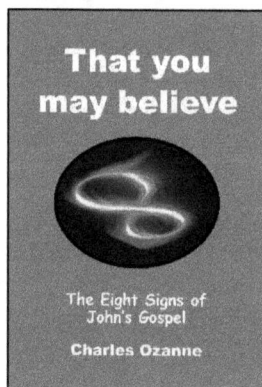

That you may believe

The Eight Signs of John's Gospel

Charles Ozanne

The Signs in John's Gospel

(A Study of Christ's Public Ministry)
by W M Henry

At the end of his gospel John tells us the reason why he wrote his gospel and why he based it around the miraculous signs performed by the Lord Jesus.

Jesus did many other miraculous signs in the presence of his disciples, which are not recorded in this book. But these are written that you may believe that Jesus is the Christ, the Son of God, and that by believing you may have life in his name. (John 20:30-31)

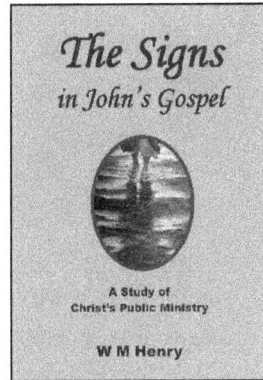

If the signs occupy such a central role, then we need to appreciate what they signified. To do that we need to understand their effect upon the people who witnessed them, the Jewish Nation. How did they react to these miraculous signs? What did they say about them? And what did they do about them?

These two books are available as paperbacks from
www.obt.org.uk

and from

The Open Bible Trust, Fordland Mount,
Upper Basildon, Reading, RG8 8LU, UK.

They are also available as eBooks from Amazon and Apple and as KDP paperbacks from Amazon.

About the Author

Brian Sherring was born in Isleworth, Middlesex, England in 1932. Following a technical education, he took an engineering apprenticeship and worked for some years as a design draughtsman in agricultural engineering. He was onetime Assistant Principal of The Chapel of the Opened Book in London and wrote regular articles for *The Berean Expositor* and several booklets. He then spent some 25 years in the food import business and worked with farm animals at weekends as a hobby. He lives with his wife in retirement in Surrey and is now a regular contributor *Search* magazine.

He has written many Bible Study Booklets and the following five major books:

- *Paul's Letter to the Romans: Background & Introduction*
- *The Mystery of Ephesians*
- *Messiah and His People.*
- *The Ten Commandments*
- *The Holy Spirit and His Ministry through the Scriptures*

More information on these five books is given on the next pages.

Information about the numerous Bible Study Booklets written by Brian Sherring can be seen on **www.obt.org.uk** (the website of The Open Bible Trust) or you can use this url:

http://www.obt.org.uk/brian-sherring

The Holy Spirit and His Ministry through the Scriptures

By Brian Sherring

Initially the author examines the role of the Spirit in regard to *all* mankind, believers or otherwise, for His ministry involves not just Christians but mankind in general.

The author goes on to show that what has been revealed of the Spirit in the Bible develops and as we move chronologically through the pages of Scripture. We find His ministry changes according to God's plan and purpose and it is the failure to notice these changes which has caused much confusion in Christendom with respect to the work of the Holy Spirit.

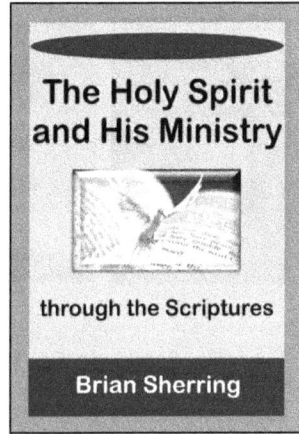

Also by Brian Sherring

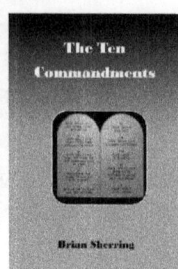

Paul's Letter to the Romans:
Background & Introduction

This book sets Paul's letter to the Romans in the context of both the New Testament and his other letters. It gives the reader a good basis for a detailed study of the epistle.

It was written from Greece some three years before Paul arrived in Rome (Acts 20:2-3). This means that it was written *before* the judgement Paul pronounced upon the Jewish leaders in Rome (Acts 28:25-28). That is *before* Paul wrote Ephesians and Colossians in which new teachings are revealed about a heavenly calling, about Gentile and Jewish equality, and about the abolishment of the Law of Moses. It is essential when reading Romans, not to read back into it such teaching as these, and the author does an excellent job of explaining Romans in its correct historical context.

The Mystery of Ephesians

In Ephesians 3:3 Paul mentions a 'mystery', and states that he had written about it briefly, i.e. earlier in the letter. So … What is this 'mystery'? … Why have so few Christians heard about it? … And why do some, who have heard about it, reject it? … Even oppose it?

With great clarity, Brian Sherring explains that the Greek word translated 'mystery' does not mean something 'mysterious' but refers to a 'secret', and this 'secret' is an important one. It relates to all mankind, and God had just revealed it to Paul and wanted Paul to make it known far and wide ... which is just what he did in writing Ephesians.

Messiah and His People

In this book, Brian Sherring takes the reader through the Bible and the unfolding portrait it paints of the Messiah, the Christ, the Redeemer.

He starts off in Genesis 3, where we learn of the seed of the woman who is to crush the serpent's head, and as we progress through time, slowly more and more is revealed about this One. He is to descend from Abraham and be of the house of David. He is to be born of a virgin and be born in Bethlehem.

He is to combine the offices of Prophet, Priest and King. From Ephesians 1 we learn that in the end He is to be head over all things and Philippians 2 states He is to have that Name which is above every name.

The Ten Commandments

In spite of an increasing lack of knowledge of the Bible in Britain, the Ten Commandments are probably still the best-known set of laws in the western society. They lie behind our justice system and, in Christian society, form an outline of what God requires of mankind. They are of course, only an outline, or skeleton, that needs to be expanded—and that is just what this book does.

****

The books on the previous pages are available as perfect bound paperbacks from

www.obt.org.uk

and from

The Open Bible Trust, Fordland Mount,
Upper Basildon, Reading, RG8 8LU, UK.

They are also available as eBooks from Amazon and Apple
and as KDP paperbacks from Amazon.

Further Reading

Brian Sherring is a regular contributor to

Search magazine

**For a free sample of
the Open Bible Trust's magazine Search,
please email**

admin@obt.org.uk

or visit

www.obt.org.uk/search

Bibliography

Beasley-Murray George R. *Commentary on John's Gospel* WBC.

Bullinger E.W. *The Seven Sayings to the Woman at the Well* (OBT reprint).

The Companion Bible. Appendix 176.

Number in Scripture

Common Prayer Book of.

Edersheim Alfred *Life and Times of Jesus the Messiah* Longmans Green.

Eusebius *Ecclesiastical History* Loeb Classical Library Harvard UP.

Farrar Austin *The Revelation of St John the Divine* Oxford Press.

Fohrer Georg *History of Israelite Religion* transl. By Davie E. Green SPCK.

Greek-English Interlinear New Testament Tyndale House.

Hagner D.A. *Commentary on Ezekiel WBC.*

The Holy Land, various modern guides.

Josephus *Antiquities of The Jews* transl.by William Whiston, Thos.Nelson.

Lewis C.S. *The Problem of Pain.*

Liddell and Scott *Greek-English Lexicon.*

Lightfoot J.B. *Biblical Essays* Macmillan.

Moffatt James *The Moffatt Translation of the Bible.*

The Gospel of John Moffatt N.T. Commentaries Hodder & Stoughton.

Introduction to the Literature of the New Testament T & T Clark.

New Bible Dictionary IVP.

Penny Michael *40 Problem Passages* OBT.

The Miracles of the Apostles OBT.

Galatians: *Interpretation and Application* OBT.

Penny Michael and Sylvia *Resurrection When*? OBT.

Robinson John A.T. *Redating The New Testament* SCM.

    The Priority of John SCM.

Sacks Jonathan Chief Rabbi Lord *Future Tense*: *A Vision for Jews* Hodder.

    The Great Partnership Hodder.

The Septuagint (*LXX*) Greek translation of O.T.

Sherring Brian. *The Gospel of John and the Samaritans* OBT.

    The Mystery of Ephesians OBT.

    Paul's Letter to the Romans: Background and Introduction OBT.

    The Ten Commandments OBT.

    The Book of Job: *Suffering and the Deep Things of God* OBT.

Stern David H. *The Complete Jewish Bible.*

    Jewish New Testament Commentary.

Tasker R.V.G. *Tyndale New Testament Commentaries.*

Welch C.H. *Life Through His Name* Berean Publishing Trust.

    The Berean Expositor Volume 20 1930.

Westcott B.F. *The Gospel according to St John.*

Wikipedia (Google).

Young's Literal Version of the Bible

About this Book

A Book of Signs
The Miraculous Signs in the Gospel of John

The author of each Gospel had a reason why he wrote and recorded what he did. In the case of the Gospel of John, the author states that he has recorded a selected number of "signs", from "the innumerable signs" that Jesus did "in the presence of His disciples," to convince his readers that:

> Jesus is the Christ (Messiah), the Son of God, and that by believing you may have life in his name. (John 20:31)

This was why John wrote his Gospel and this was the goal he hoped to achieve, but why these particular *signs* and how do they show that Jesus is the Messiah and the Son of God? These are the two main issues dealt with in this excellent book.

****